SPIRITUAL STEWARDSHIP

Stephen Kaung

ISBN: 978-1-942521-42-6

Available from:

Christian Testimony Ministry
4424 Huguenot Road
Richmond, Virginia 23235

www.christiantestimonyministry.com

Printed in USA

CONTENTS

THE STEWARD

Luke 12:35-48—Let your loins be girded about, and lamps burning; and ye like men who wait their own lord whenever he may leave the wedding, that when he comes and knocks, they may open to him immediately. Blessed are those bondmen whom the lord on coming shall find watching; verily I say unto you, that he will gird himself and make them recline at table, and coming up will serve them. And if he come in the second watch, and come in the third watch, and find them thus, blessed are those bondmen. But this know, that if the master of the house had known in what hour the thief was coming, he would have watched, and not have suffered his house to be dug through. And ye therefore, be ye ready, for in the hour in which ye do not think it, the Son of man comes. And Peter said to him, Lord, sayest thou this parable to us, or also to all? And the Lord said, Who then is the faithful and prudent steward, whom his lord will set over his household, to give the measure of corn in season?

Blessed is that bondman whom his lord on coming shall find doing thus; verily I say unto you, that he will set him over all that he has. But if that bondman should say in his heart, My lord delays to come, and begin to beat the menservants and the maidservants, and to eat and to drink and to be drunken, the lord of that bondman shall come in a day when he does not expect it, and in an hour he knows not of, and shall cut him in two and appoint his portion with the unbelievers. But that bondman who knew his own lord's will, and had not prepared himself nor done his will, shall be beaten with many stripes; but he who knew it not, and did things worthy of stripes, shall be beaten with few. And to every one to whom much has been given, much shall be required from him; and to whom men have committed much, they will ask from him the more.

I Corinthians 4:1-2—Let a man so account of us as servants of Christ, and stewards of the mysteries of God. Here, further, it is sought in stewards, that a man be found faithful.

Let's have a word of prayer:

Dear Lord, we want to thank Thee for gathering us together. We do gather in the name of our beloved Lord, and we fully believe that Thou art faithful and Thy presence is now with us. Dear Lord, we do realize we are standing on holy ground. We will remove our shoes, stand in our rightful place, look up to Thee and say, Lord, what has Thou to say to us? Thy servants are here listening. Speak, Lord, and work until Thy will is done, to the praise of Thy glory. We ask in the name of our Lord Jesus Christ. Amen.

Thank God for gathering us together once again. I always feel it is a rare opportunity that God's people in this day can come and seek the face of the Lord together. I always feel it is mercy, and He is merciful to us.

STEWARDS OF THE MYSTERIES OF GOD

The text of this conference is taken from Luke 12:42. Our Lord is here asking a question: "Who then is the faithful and prudent steward, whom his lord will set over his household, to give the measure of corn in season?"

Our Lord Jesus oftentimes answers a question with a question. Actually, here it is Peter who is asking a question and he says, "Lord, are You speaking to us, the apostles, or are You speaking to all?" And out Lord answered him with another question: "Who then is the faithful and prudent steward, whom the Lord will set over His household, to give the measure of corn in season?" If you read the context you will find that our Lord Jesus was talking about His return. He is challenging us to gird up our loins and keep our lamps burning, waiting diligently for the Lord to come back from the wedding. He will come back and knock, and whoever answers the door, immediately the Lord will come in and He will serve them. And the Lord said, "If you know when the thief is coming you will be watchful, and you will not allow him to come without notice." So when our Lord was using this parable, Peter asked the question: "Whom are you referring to? Do you mean that we, the apostles, are the stewards of the mysteries of God? Do you mean that we are to keep ourselves always ready, alert, watchful, waiting, and when you come back, we open the door immediately? Or are you referring to the multitudes, to those people who are here listening?"

And our Lord Jesus gave him the answer with another question. I think if you read the question and the parable that follows, it is evident that our Lord Jesus is not referring to just the apostles; it is to all. In other words, it is to every one of the redeemed. We are all stewards of the household of God, and we are supposed to be always ready, always watching, always waiting, never in any sense letting up, going to sleep, or even beating our fellow bondmen and getting drunk.

Brothers and sisters, here is something that is applied to every one of us. We are in the last days. The Lord has promised that He is coming, and His coming is imminent. He may come at any time. He may come in the second watch which is from 9:00 in the evening to 12:00 midnight. Or He may come at the third watch which is from midnight to 3:00 in the morning. He may come at any time. I think we all believe in the coming of our Lord Jesus. As we look around the world, as we look upon the situation we are living in today, it is a dangerous day, a day of testing, of trial. Things cannot be worse than what we have experienced in our day. The end is approaching.

The Lord is able to come at any moment. Some people feel that the Lord will not come until certain signs are fulfilled. May I tell you that all the signs that foretell the coming of the Lord have been fulfilled. There are signs still to be fulfilled but they will be at the coming and after the coming of the Lord. Strictly speaking, we are approaching midnight. He may come at any moment. It may be today. Thank God, if it is today! But are we ready? Are we girded up spiritually? Is the lamp within us burning? Or do we think that the Lord has delayed His coming? He will not be coming now. It may be ten years from now. There is plenty of time to get ready. So just go on with your own life, seeking the things that you think are important to you, and hopefully, at the right moment you will wake up when He comes.

But our Lord Jesus said, "At the time you think He delays, at the time you know not of, He comes." So we do feel the urgency of our time.

We do not have much time left for us to fulfill the stewardship that He has given to us. If that is the case, do you not think it is time for us to wake up and really mean business with the Lord and surrender our whole being to Him? It is the time to no longer live for our petty plans but to daily live for Him, waiting for Him, doing His bidding, being faithful, and knowing His will. So that is the reason why we feel very much burdened with this matter of spiritual stewardship.

God willing I would like to share with you dear brothers and sisters very simply on the steward. And if it is the Lord's will and we still have time we will share next time on the stewardship.

Does God Need Stewards?

I want to ask a question. Does God need stewards? Our God is the almighty God. He is the one who created the universe. He is not only the one who is able to create but He is able to manage. Our Lord Jesus is the One entrusted with the creation of the universe. All things were created in Him, by Him, and for Him. But the Bible also tells us that all things subsist in Him.

In other words, after they are created they are being held together by Him. He manages the universe. He is the Lord of the universe. He is in full control. He does not need any help. He knows everything. You remember the Bible tells us that two sparrows cost a penny, but if you have two pennies you can get five sparrows. In other words, the fifth one is added in without any cost; it is worthless. And yet our Lord Jesus said, "Your heavenly Father does not permit even that odd sparrow to fall to the ground forgotten by Him." How many hairs do you have on your head? Who has counted them? But our God has not only counted your hairs but He has numbered them, and when you combed your hair this morning, number so and so fell off.

Do you think God needs stewards? I feel He has no need for stewards, for managers to manage things for Him because He is well able to do everything without anybody else. And in a sense, if somebody else comes in and helps, it gives Him more trouble.

Have you thought about this? Does God need any stewards to manage His household, His estate? I believe that we all know that He does not need it but He does it. Why is it so? This is just like Him. Our God is love, and because He is love He wants to give. Because He loves He wants to draw people in. Because He loves He wants to have people share with Him, not only in His blessing but also in His responsibility. Think of that!

SHARING IN GOD'S WORK

We think more of blessing. I believe every morning we wake up and say, "Lord, bless me because without Your blessing I cannot go through this day." And it is true. But do we ever think of saying when we wake up in the morning, "Lord, what responsibility do you want to share with me that I should do in order to fulfill Your heart's desire?" Probably we never say such a thing, never even thought of such a thing because we think, "He is almighty, all sufficient, El Shaddai; so let Him do everything." We just enjoy and enjoy and enjoy and be selfish and self-centered and live for ourselves.

Brothers and sisters, has the Holy Spirit ever reminded us that God wants us to be like Him?

He wants us to take up not only His life but also His character. This is the will of God and because He is the One who always wants to share, therefore He calls stewards to His household to manage His estate as if it depends upon us. Isn't that marvelous? I feel that blessing is marvelous. Who doesn't want blessing? The more the better. But do we ever think that responsibility is something more than just blessing?

Or may I put it another way. It is the blessing of all blessing that God should draw us to share His work with Him, to share His responsibility with Him, to bring about, as it were, the fulfillment of His eternal purpose. What a privilege! What an honor that He has bestowed upon us! Unfortunately, how we fail Him! God created man in the garden of Eden. As the Bible says, "He created man in His own image after His likeness." And immediately after He created them, He also said, "Let man have dominion over the fowls of the air, the living things on earth, and the fishes of the sea." Is it not from the very beginning of the creation of man that God has made known His mind to us?

MAN CREATED IN GOD'S IMAGE

Why is it that God should create man in His own image after His likeness? He has never done that to any other creature, only to man. He wants to share His life with man. The mountains cannot receive His life. They manifest His magnitude, His power. The animals cannot receive His life. They depend upon Him for their livelihood. It is only man, created after God's own image, who has the capacity to receive the very life of God into their lives, but giving that life to man means something. It means that you are to have dominion over what God has created. God created everything Himself, but God wants man to govern all that He has created. This is what God purposed in the very beginning, but unfortunately, man failed God. Instead of having dominion over the created things to subdue them for God, to bring everything back to the will of God, to the feet of Christ, man himself succumbed to temptation. Man failed; he sinned against God, not only in the sense of helping God, but he created more trouble for God. That is what we are. But thank God, He never changes. He is the same yesterday, today, and forever.

11

Once His mind is made up, no matter what happens, He will see it through gloriously.

What did God do? He sent His only beloved Son into this world to be a Man. This is the great mystery. The Word became flesh, tabernacled among men, full of grace and truth. God's purpose for man has never changed. Man has failed God but God never fails man. What He has in His heart to do, He will do it. So He sent His beloved Son into this world to be a Man, and as a Man, how He fulfilled His stewardship! All through His life He gave Himself totally to God. He took upon Himself the form of a bondslave. He was obedient to God even unto death, and that the death of the cross. On the cross of Calvary He shouted: "It is finished!" The mission was fulfilled. What God had entrusted to man is now made possible. It has been proven in *the* Man, the Son of Man, our Lord Jesus Christ. And having put His life in us, the life of the Son of God, Son of Man, He made every provision for us to fulfill our stewardship. Isn't that marvelous?

STEWARDSHIP IS FOR ALL

In the first letter of Paul to the Corinthian believers in 4:1 he said, "Let a man so account of us as servants of Christ, and stewards of the mysteries of God." When you read this verse, it may give you the impression that the stewardship of the mysteries of God is limited to the apostles or to those who are called to work for Him because we know that I Corinthians was written by the apostle Paul. But he did not write this letter alone; he always tried to draw in someone with him, to stand together with him and send out this letter. It is so much like God in this life of Paul.

So in the beginning of the letter, he said, "Paul, the apostle and the brother Sosthenes..." In other words, you find the apostle Paul and with him that brother Sosthenes. He said, "Let a man so account of us..." At least it refers to the two of them, and as you read this book of Corinthians, you know that the *us* here is really more than Paul and Sosthenes because he mentions Apollos, Peter, and other people. So when we first read this, we may think the stewardship is given only to the apostles and those specially called by God, that they are the stewards of the mysteries of God, but this is not so.

In Ephesians 3:9-11 it says, "And to enlighten all with the knowledge of what is the administration of the mystery hidden throughout the ages in God, who has created all things, in order that now to the principalities and authorities in the heavenlies might be made known through the church the all-various wisdom of God, according to the purpose of the ages, which he purposed in Christ Jesus our Lord."

GOD HAS A SECRET

Now it is true, the mystery of God, which is Christ, was revealed to the prophets and apostles because it is a mystery. God has mysteries, secrets. Do you have secrets? God has secrets, and He has kept His secret so well that even this secret was formed in Him before the foundation of the world before He created the heavens and the earth. In eternity past when God existed by Himself, He had a secret, and that secret was made according to His good pleasure. In other words, His secret does not come from anywhere else because there was nobody else. His secret came from Himself and this is His good pleasure. It pleases Him; that is the thing that He likes, and He formed that secret even before the foundation of the world. And it is upon this secret, this mystery that He began to work all things. All His counsels are based upon His secret, and we call this secret the eternal purpose of God. In other words, God has a purpose and He made that purpose before He did anything, and everything that He does is according to that purpose. And He will see to it that this purpose will be fully realized so that He may be glorified.

Here you find we are touching something. We are often so limited, so small that everything we touch is just me or mine, I, my family, my things. That is all we have, but our God is infinite. He is rich—the unsearchable riches of Christ.

This secret that God has in His heart is so dear to Him. It means everything to Him. He wants to see that secret finally become a reality, and He has been working from eternity through time towards that purpose. Just think! If we are being connected with that secret of God, if we are being drawn into that eternal purpose of God, we will burst; we cannot contain ourselves. Why should we be so bothered with our petty self, knowing that He has called us into some tremendous, infinite, purpose of God, even His heart's desire, and we are involved in it? Now will you please forget your petty little plan and get into His immense plan that God may be glorified. Think of that!

Brothers and sisters, I do not know how to contain myself. From the day of His creation God has been working out His purpose even though it has been frustrated time and again. Even in the former world of the angels and the spirits He created, Lucifer and one third of the angelic hosts rebelled against His purpose. But He did not give up; He continued to work on. As a matter of fact, every seeming failure to Him is a step forward. That is the way God works. He created man a little lower than the angels, and yet man surpassed the angels. Man fell into the hands of the fallen angel, but through our Lord

Jesus He redeemed man. He redeemed us who are worth nothing, less than nothing, worse than nothing. Yet He gave us His own life, and He saw to it that the life would grow and not just remain babes in Christ. This is not God's purpose for us. He wants us to grow in that life from little children in Christ Jesus to young people in Christ Jesus to fathers in Christ Jesus. Why should we grow? Why spiritual growth? Why not stay in babyhood? Probably for many of us we like our babyhood more than any other time. What if I remained a baby for a hundred years? Wouldn't that be wonderful? I have no responsibility, always being helped, always being supplied, always being taken care of, and whatever I want I would just cry and do it. But where is God's purpose?

THE ALL-VARIOUS WISDOM OF GOD

Oh, brothers and sisters, may we be purpose-oriented and not need-oriented. As long as we are need-oriented we remain babes. We have to outgrow it, and God wants us to grow into sons and daughters so that we may be placed as sons, sonship. Sonship and stewardship are closely related. The more you grow in Christ Jesus, the more His character is built in you, the more you are able to be a greater part in that mystery of God, and the more you are able to serve Him in the right way instead of doing disservice to Him. Through the apostles and the prophets the secret is now made known to us. And after we have known this secret what should we do? The Bible says, "Even the principalities and the authorities will learn wisdom, the all-various wisdom of God through the church, the body of Christ." We often say the angels are more intelligent than we are. That is true, but do you know we can be more intelligent than the angels? Even the angels have to learn from us the all-various wisdom of God.

I Peter 1 tells us the same thing. Not only are the prophets looking into this salvation that Christ has prepared for us but even the angels like to know how fallen man who is lower than the angels, fallen even lower, and yet God can raise them up, put life in them, give character to them, give them responsibility, and by the grace of God are able to fulfill their stewardship. That is the all-various wisdom of God. The angels never have that, and they are looking at the church to see how the church reveals even this to the angels. Isn't that all too marvelous for us?

Even though Paul and Sosthenes are considered as the stewards of the mysteries of God, because they have passed this mystery on to us, the church, the body of Christ, every member of the body of Christ, therefore this stewardship is to us all. Do not forget your stewardship. Last year, when we were here together, we talked about this matter of spiritual sonship, and if you have really heard it, I believe that throughout the year you wanted to grow to be sons. You want to be placed as sons by your heavenly Father. You desire that He will notice you, pay attention to you, always thinking of you, helping you to see that you really grow up into sons that He may place you as sons into His responsibility. But do you know that sonship and stewardship are inseparable? Son speaks of life, divine life, spiritual life, the life of Christ. Steward speaks of service, responsibility. Son may speak of privilege; steward speaks of responsibility. And these two things always go together.

LOVESLAVES

The apostle Paul shows us how we can be stewards of the mysteries of God. In I Corinthians 4:1 it says, "Let a man so account of us as servants of Christ, and stewards of the mysteries of God." Before this matter of stewards he first put servants. We are both, but if you are not a servant you cannot be a steward. Now we know that in the New Testament in the Greek there are several words that are used to describe servant. One word that is used means bondman; you are a slave. Now we do not want to be slaves, but thank God when you come to the family of God, we want to be slaves. We are slaves, bondslaves, loveslaves. And this word *servant* is a special word. In the original, the background of this word is *under-rower*. In the old days you do not have steam engines or steamboats, so all these boats, ships, galleys are being rowed in order to go wherever they are going. In these boats there are a number of people who are rowing and they are called under-rowers. In the old days the rowers were usually slaves, chained in the bottom of the boat. They were there to row the boat any where it wanted to go. And they were under the command of the one who was beating the drum. When he beat the drum, then they would row together in unison; there would be no discord. If one rowed this way and another rowed that way the boat would go nowhere, so they had to row as one under the command of the person at the drum. Their position was very low, way below the sailors. They were slaves, with no liberty of their own, and they were completely under command. Then the boat would go maybe from Europe to Asia or somewhere else and do the job.

So who are we? So far as our life is concerned we are sons and daughters of God. Wonderful! But at the same time, we are slaves, bought with a price. We are loveslaves. We do not want to go out free. We love our Master and His household. We are both sons and under-rowers. That is what we are. It is just like our Lord Jesus, who is the Son of God, yet He put on the form of a bondslave. Only son-servant can fulfill stewardship. Christ is the Son-Servant. He fulfills the stewardship, and by His grace we as son-servants are able to fulfill our stewardship.

After we receive the life of Christ, after His love has called us and constrained us, have we really surrendered voluntarily, willingly, fully and absolutely as we know how? Have we surrendered to our Lord Jesus as our Commander, as our Lord, so that we may row together under His command in unison? If there is anything in any one of us that thinks he is master of himself, we will spoil the purpose of God, and we can never row together under command. So we have a tremendous responsibility. Where are we?

THE UNRIGHTEOUS STEWARD

In Luke 16, we find the parable of the unrighteous steward. The steward of the household wastes away the property of the master. The property is so immense. Abraham had so many sheep, so many cattle, so many properties that he had a chief steward to manage his affairs. Now a steward is one who manages the affairs and the estate of the household of his master. He does not own the property, but he manages according to the will of the master. Everything is supplied by the master. He is supposed to be faithful and prudent in dispensing the food in measure and in season. But this unrighteous steward used his master's property to benefit himself. He was an unrighteous steward, and one day the reckoning would come.

So if we are not faithful in what He has entrusted to us today, as the Bible says, who will give more to you? Who will give you that which is your own (see Luke 16:12)? This is the time, the only time that we can prove our stewardship. If we do not do it now, when the Lord returns and He reckons with us, the time is gone. The opportunity is gone. So thank God, we do not know how long our time will be, but we know as long as it is today, this is the time that we should be faithful and prudent, faithful in the sense of giving our all to it, prudent in the sense of knowing the mind of the Master.

THE PARABLES OF THE MINAS

In the Bible you find many parables that are connected with this. For instance, in Luke 19, the nobleman was going away to receive his kingdom and he gave his property to his ten bondslaves. Every one got a mina, about one sixtieth of a talent. And they are given equally because mina here speaks of the grace of God. In the family of God, the grace of God is entrusted to every one of us equally. You may think certain brothers and sisters seem to receive more grace than you do but not so. So far as grace is concerned, it is equal. Why is it that some people manifest more grace and other people do not? It depends upon your faithfulness. We are all given one mina but some produce ten minas, some five minas, and some just one mina because they are lazy. They wrap it up in a handkerchief, no sweating, put it in the earth, thinking they have kept all but they lose all.

THE TALENTS

Then in Matthew 25 there are the talents. There are three servants—one, five talents, one, two talents, one, one talent. In other words, they speak of gifts. God gives gifts according to our capacity, and if we do according to our capacity, then we will hear, "Well done, come and enjoy the joy of the Lord." But the one with one talent buried it. How many of God's people today bury their talent! What a pity.

THE FAITHFUL SERVANT

When you read Matthew 24, you find the same parable as Luke 12. Our Lord said, "Who is the faithful and prudent servant to whom the master has set over his household to give the corn in measure and in season?" The same person can be the wicked one or he can be the faithful one. It all depends upon how you respond to it.

Oh, brothers and sisters, we are all stewards. He has entrusted Himself to us, each according to our capacity, and yet we all are responsible. Are we faithful and wise in managing His affairs? If so, when He shall come back, we will welcome Him with joy. We will hear the voice, "Good, faithful, and prudent servant. Come and enjoy the joy of the Lord."

THE UNFAITHFUL SERVANT

But if we are not, the discipline will be severe. God disciplines His children. He does not punish us; He disciplines us. If we do not receive discipline today, when He shall return, there will still be discipline. And if you read the Scripture you will find that it can be very severe, cut into two, as if you are an unbeliever. But that does not mean you will lose your salvation. You will lose the kingdom, the thousand years of reigning and ruling with Christ. But thank God, God never fails. When eternity shall come, all will be sons, all will be faithful and prudent servants. Their names will be upon their foreheads, and they shall see Him every day. Glory!

Let us pray:

Dear Lord, we do want to praise and thank Thee. How great, how marvelous, how wonderful, how glorious is Thy purpose, and Thou should involve us. Oh Lord, do not allow us to become complacent. Do not allow us to sit back. We pray that Thou will gird up our loins that our lamp may be burning and at Thy knocking, immediately, we will open the door. Welcome; come, Lord Jesus. Amen.

STEWARDSHIP

I Corinthians 4:1-2—Let a man so account of us as servants of Christ, and stewards of the mysteries of God. Here, further, it is sought in stewards, that a man be found faithful.

Let us pray:

Dear Lord as we gather here, we sense Thou has brought us into Thy inner chamber, and there we behold Thy beauty. We partake of Thy life. We enter into Thy secret counsel, and there we have heard Thy call: "Come, take up thy stewardship of the mysteries of God in My household." Oh Lord, we answer Thy call and come. We look to Thee to reveal Thy mind to us. We depend upon Thy grace to enable us to be faithful and prudent stewards of Thine, and for this end we trust ourselves to Thee. May Thy will be done in our lives, may Thy kingdom come, and may Thy name be hallowed in the midst of Thy own. We give Thee all the glory; in the precious name of our Lord Jesus. Amen.

I do hope that these two simple verses in I Corinthians 4 will really be deeply inscribed upon each of our hearts. Thank God, for calling all of us. It is not just the apostles, not just a few, but all the redeemed of the Lord, all who have His life in them that are called. We are all called into the household of God to take part in the management of that house. Therefore we need to realize that each and every one of us is a steward; not just a steward of any kind but a steward of God's eternal purpose. We are stewards of God's household and stewards of God's estate. What an honor, and yet what a responsibility!

We have spoken especially on this matter of the steward, and now we want to look together into this matter of stewardship. Steward speaks of the person who is called by God to take part in the management of His interest, and we are all called into that. Even though we may have different gifts, even though we are apportioned to different responsibilities, let us remember that it is not just a single gift or a special appointment or a special work that we are involved with. We must remember that even though our gifts may be different, our places in the house of God may be different, our responsibility may be specific, yet we are all together as stewards in the household of God. In other words, we need a more comprehensive over-all vision or understanding of what we are entrusted with. So we would like to enter into this matter of stewardship.

Steward speaks of person; stewardship speaks of the responsibility. We are all stewards, and we are all in stewardship. But we need to understand what it is that God has entrusted to us, what is our stewardship. Is it just a specific work of one kind? Is it that we are all serving God each in our own way, even though we may be faithful in that particular area? What we forget is that we are all involved in one stewardship. There is an over-all understanding that we must have. Otherwise, we will be each doing our own work. We may be faithful to that particular work, but it is all separated, individual, independent, not related, not together. So I feel that we need to have a real understanding of what stewardship is.

The apostle Paul tells us that we are stewards of the mysteries of God. This is what our stewardship is. Our stewardship is neither our particular gift nor our particular work. Our stewardship is the mysteries of God. It is something far greater, far more comprehensive than what we usually think.

THE GREAT COMMISSION

When we talk about stewardship, what is your real understanding? We are familiar with Matthew 28:18-20, that great commission. You remember that before our Lord Jesus left He gave us a great commission. He said, "All power has been given me in heaven and upon earth. Go therefore and make disciples of all the nations, baptizing them to the name of the Father, and of the Son, and of the Holy Spirit; teaching them to observe all things whatsoever I have enjoined you. And behold, I am with you all the days, until the completion of the age."

When you read this great commission, what is your understanding? I think when most people hear of this great commission that our Lord Jesus committed the church to do, we usually think of evangelism. "Go to the nations and evangelize them. Bring them into the salvation of the Lord." That is the great commission most people understand. And thank God, throughout the generations, for two thousand years the church has been trying to fulfill that great commission. We feel that we are called to go to the nations, evangelize them, bring them out of hell into heaven, and then our stewardship is done. Thank God for that. I can never thank God enough for the missionaries who came to China and brought the glad tidings to us. It is great. It is necessary. It is important. But if you read very carefully this great commission, you will find there is not a word about evangelizing. That does not mean that evangelizing is not important; it is very important because without that how can you disciple all nations? Thank God, the church has heard and has undertaken this great commission. That is the beginning, and for this we are most thankful. But everybody who reads this great commission can see that it is far more than just evangelizing.

The Lord said, "Go to the nations; disciple all nations." When our Lord Jesus was on earth, He preached the kingdom of God: "Believe Him and you shall be saved, born from above, and you shall enter into the kingdom of God." But at the same time, while he was preaching He was calling for disciples. He was discipling the nations.

What is discipling? It simply means "follow Him, learn of Him, be like Him." It is not just to be saved but saved to be like Him, taking His character upon them; growing up into sons. That is what discipling means.

BAPTISM

"Baptizing them in the name of the Father, the Son, and the Holy Spirit." Why is baptism so important? It is important because this is the beginning of true discipleship. It is the door by which you enter into being disciples of our Lord Jesus.

In the old days we do not have schools like we have today. So when you want to learn something, you have to be an apprentice, and when you become an apprentice you do not stay at home. You leave your old environment behind. You leave your home, you leave your family, you leave your past, and you stay with your master to be one of his family. Usually, during the first year, if you are going to learn carpentry your master will not even let you touch the instruments. He will ask you to hold his baby, serve him at his meals, sweep the floor, and do all these things. It seems as if it has nothing to do with what you have come to learn. Gradually he will allow you to touch the instruments and teach you something. Why? It is because he is discipling you. He will not only teach you his skill, which is secondary; he will teach you how to behave, how to be a man. That is the most important thing.

Oftentimes, after you have been with your master for three years or more you not only learn all his skills as a master carpenter, but you learn his way. You begin to walk like your master; you talk like your master; you think like your master. You are like a duplicate of your master. Then you are graduated. That is the way of Christ with us. He saved us in order to disciple us. "Come and follow Me." You find that the disciples left everything and followed Him. They were with Him day and night. They heard Him, watched Him, stayed with Him, and abode with Him. And it all begins with our being baptized to the name of the Father, the Son, and the Holy Spirit.

What is baptism? Baptism is not just a ritual. Some people ask the question: "If I believe in the Lord Jesus and am saved, what else is needed? The water will never cleanse me from my sins. It is the blood of the Lord Jesus. So why should I be baptized?" But baptism is important because it tells us that all our past is dead, buried, and now I rise up from the water, alive in Christ Jesus. I am being delivered from my past. It is no longer I; it is Christ who lives in me. That is the beginning. But only in that way are you able to be taught of all the things that our Lord Jesus has commanded us. Otherwise, if He tries to teach you anything and you have your own idea, you will say, "My idea is better. I will stick to my former ways." You will never learn. You have to be dead to the past, dead to yourself, completely new, walk in newness of life with a new mind transformed. That is how you can be taught, and you can learn and really be like Christ.

And our Lord Jesus said, "And I will be with you to the end of the ages." What is the great commission that He has given to the church? Why is it that we must be discipled? Why is it that we must be baptized? Why is it that we must learn all that He has taught us? What is His purpose? The Lord said, "You are Peter. On this rock I will build my church, and the gates of Hades will not prevail against it. You are a little stone, a piece of the rock. Now you have life in you, and you need to be built upon Me. And you need to be built with other small stones into My house, into My church, and the gates of Hades will not prevail against it."

So what is the great commission? The great commission is that we are called to take up the stewardship of the mysteries of God. This is our great commission. Anything less than that is below and is shut off from the eternal purpose of God.

A LARGE VISION

When we come to this matter of stewardship, I think first of all we need to realize what a stewardship that is. He so loves us that He commits Himself totally to us. Our God, our Lord does not just commit a little bit of Himself to us;

He has committed Himself totally to us. All the mysteries of God, all the secrets of God, all that is in the very heart of God, all that God has according to His good pleasure purposed since the foundation of the world, all that He has been working throughout the time, all that He is aiming at, He commits to the church. He commits to us. His commitment is total and our stewardship is total. So we need a larger vision.

Somebody asked me this question: "If I know what my gift is, if I am faithful to the gift that God has given me, if I am doing my bit of work as I understand it, do I still need vision? Do I still need a larger understanding?" Certainly you do. Otherwise, what you are doing is independent, is individual. It is not serving the whole counsel of God. So it is absolutely important that when we come to this matter of stewardship, first of all we need an understanding. Even though we are doing our little bit, that little bit is not isolated, it is not a work by itself, it is not our objective. It is a part of the greater plan of God. It is a part in the eternal purpose of God. It is a part of the mysteries of God. Now if you see it I wonder how you will react.

Do you see that we are involved in something so immense, so eternal, so spiritual, so all-inclusive. Even the mysteries of God have been entrusted to us. We are to keep, we are to possess, we are to serve, we are to fulfill, to realize. What a stewardship that is! Do not think that it is a little bit of work that God has entrusted to you. Even though it may be small in human eyes, it is a part of the mysteries of God that God has entrusted to the church and to each and every one of us. So first of all we need to ask the Lord to really open our understanding. Grant us the spirit of wisdom and revelation that we may really know Him. Without that all our works will be in vain. We may think we are serving God but we may be like Saul of Tarsus doing God a great disservice. It was not until on the road to Damascus that he saw the Lord and it changed his ministry.

FOUR ASPECTS OF THE MYSTERIES OF GOD

So we would like to go into this matter of the stewardship of the mysteries of God. You notice here that the apostle Paul talked about the mysteries of God. It simply means God's secrets.

God has called us into His inner chamber and there He will reveal His secrets to us. He has many secrets but all these secrets are related. And we would like to share a little bit on the four-fold secret of God, four aspects of the mysteries of God to which we have all been called to manage, to keep, and to work in faithfully.

Christ—The Mystery of God

First of all in Ephesians 1:9-10: "Having made known to us the mystery of his will, according to his good pleasure which he purposed in himself for the administration of the fullness of times; to head up, [to sum up] all things in the Christ, the things in the heavens and the things upon the earth."

Colossians 2:2-3: "To the end that their hearts may be encouraged, being united together in love, and unto all riches of the full assurance of understanding, to the full knowledge of the mystery of God." A number of manuscripts follow with: "The mystery of God, even Christ, notably Christ, in which are hid all the treasures of wisdom and of knowledge."

What is the mystery of God? We are clearly being told the secret of God is none other than Christ. Christ is the mystery of God. All the fullness of the Godhead dwells in Him bodily, and we are complete in Him. In other words, if you want to know God, know Jesus. If you do not know Christ, you will never know God. God is the greatest unknown, the greatest mystery. You may search for Him but you cannot find Him. He is so infinite. He is so immense. He is so high that He is beyond any human mind, any searching by man.

You remember our Lord Jesus said, "No one knows the Son but the Father. No one knows the Father but the Son and to whom the Son has revealed Him." God is the greatest mystery in the universe, but one day that secret was out. The Word became flesh, tabernacled among men, full of grace and truth. No one has ever seen God but the Son has declared Him. All that you want to know about God is in Christ Jesus. Outside of Him there is no knowledge of God.

Philip said to the Lord: "Show us the Father and it suffices us; we are satisfied." And you know what our Lord said? He must have said it with a very sad tone: "Philip, you have seen Me. You have been with Me for so long and you still have not seen the Father? Do you not know that the Father is in Me and I am in the Father? If you see Me, you see the Father." That is the only place you can know God. The mystery is here.

Everything you want to know about God you will find in Christ. If you try to find God outside of Christ, you are lost. That is what the Colossian believers did. They believed in the Lord Jesus. They wanted to be complete; they wanted to be full. But they were being led to something other than Christ—Christ plus, and they lost it. Our Christ is One whom we need to know throughout our life, and life is too short for us to know all of Christ. Even in eternity we will continue to learn Christ because He is the infinite One. There is no end to it. Are you satisfied with the Christ that you know? As our brother Sparks often said, "You make Christ little as if you are able to comprehend Him. He is far beyond every one of us. There is always something more to learn of Him because God is infinite." And He trusts this mystery to the church.

We have received the stewardship of the mysteries of God, but what is it that we are really managing today? Christ is the mystery of God, and God has committed the testimony of Jesus to the church. We are here to bear witness to Christ Jesus. The Lord said, "You have been with me for so long, but when the Holy Spirit comes, He shall bear witness of me and you too shall bear Me witness." So we are the holder, as it were, of the testimony of Jesus.

In the book of Revelation, you find again and again it is said, "The testimony of Jesus." John the apostle was exiled to the island of Patmos for the word of God and the testimony of Jesus. And throughout the ages there have been people who have held the testimony of Jesus. Even the whole prophecy is the testimony of Jesus. We have the testimony of Jesus. Now do we really have it? We are supposed to have it, but do we really have it.

What is the testimony of Jesus? The whole Bible is the testimony of Jesus. But let us try to condense it into one or two sentences.

When John was on the island of Patmos, he had a vision of the risen Lord. "And when I saw him I fell at his feet as dead; and he laid his right hand upon me, saying, Fear not; I am the first and the last, and the living one: and I became dead, and behold, I am living to the ages of ages, and have the keys of death and of hades" (Revelation 1:17-18).

This is the testimony that our Lord Jesus testified of Himself. He said, "I am the first and the last and the living one." That refers to the past and to eternity. He is the first and He is the last. He is the first in the sense that He is the beginning of all things. He is the last in the sense that He is the end, the aim of all things. He must have the preeminence in all things. All things come by Him, through Him, and to Him. That is what He is. And He is the living one; in order words, He is life. Before Him there was no life. Outside of Him there is no life. He is the living one, the only one who lives forever more. This is the testimony of the Lord Jesus.

Is this true to us? Is He the first in our life? It is easy to say, "Lord, You are the first." But is it true? Am I first? Is my family first? Is my interest first? Or is my church first? Who is really the first in your life? Who begins everything in what you do? Does He have the preeminence in your life, in my life? Do we allow Him to begin everything? Or do we begin something and ask for His approval? He is the first.

And He is the last. Not the last one but the final one. Everything ends up with Him. It is for Him, for His glory; not for us. Who has the testimony of Jesus? It is the one who really allows Christ to be the first and to be the last and all within. And one who really knows Him as the living One, who lives by His life. That is the testimony of Jesus. The testimony of Jesus is not just a word, but there is a power, a reality behind the word.

Therefore it says in Revelation 12, "They overcome Satan by the blood of the Lamb." They are not perfect, but they know the blood of the Lamb, the power of the precious blood of our Lord Jesus.

"And the word of their testimony…" Behind their word is the reality that Christ is the first and the last in their life and they live by the life of Christ. So that word has power to overcome

Satan. That is from eternity to the time our Lord Jesus came into this world and said, "Behold, I became dead." The living One became dead. How can it be? Because the Word became flesh and tabernacled among men. He came to be the Son of Man, a new beginning, and He came for the purpose of dying on the cross on our behalf. He came to die in order that we may live. That is what He did, and that is what we have experienced. And then, "Behold, I am living to the ages of ages. He is resurrected. Hallelujah! He has gone into death, robbed death of its power, came out victorious in resurrection, and He lives forever and forever. Do we know Him? Do we know the power of His resurrection? Are we overcoming everything?

"And He holds the keys of death and Hades." The gates of Hades shall not prevail against the church. This is the testimony of Jesus, and this is the testimony that has been entrusted to us. We are the custodian, the management. We are here to see to it that we are in it, and we are faithful and prudent that many more may be brought into that same testimony. This is the stewardship of the mystery of God.

The Mystery of Christ

Ephesians 3:9-11—"And to enlighten all with the knowledge of what is the administration of the mystery hidden throughout the ages in God, who has created all things, in order that now to the principalities and authorities in the heavenlies might be made known through the church the all-various wisdom of God, according to the purpose of the ages, which he purposed in Christ Jesus our Lord."

The mystery of God is Christ. The stewardship is the testimony of Jesus. The mystery of Christ as Paul said in Ephesians 3:4: "By which, in reading it, ye can understand my intelligence in the mystery of the Christ."

What is the mystery of Christ? The mystery of Christ is the church. If you want to know Christ there is only way to know Him and that is through the church. You are not able to know God except through Christ Jesus; it is all exclusive and inclusive. The same thing is true for the world to know about Christ. It is through the church. The church opens up the mystery of Christ that the whole world may know who

Christ is, and that is the reason why the church is called *the* Christ. You find this in I Corinthians 12:12: "For even as the body is one and has many members, but all the members of the body, being many, are one body, so also is the Christ."

We often think by the description of this verse which says that the body is one and has many members, many members yet one body, it should say, "So also is the church." And that is true; it is the church. The church is the body of Christ; it is one yet has many members. Even though there are so many members it is one body under one Head, Christ Jesus. But the Spirit of God says, "So also is *the* Christ," because the church is *the* Christ. In other words, the church is none other but Christ Himself in all of us.

It is like when God prepared a bride for Adam. Adam could not find his bride in any of the living creatures, no matter how intelligent or how big they were. He could not find anyone. So God said, "I will make him a helpmate, his like." God put him to sleep. Out of Adam's side He took something and made Eve. And when Eve was brought to Adam, immediately Adam recognized:

"This is me, bone of my bone, flesh of my flesh." It is a type; the antitype is Christ and the church. When our Lord Jesus was crucified on the cross, the soldier came and thrust his spear through His side into His heart, and out of that broken heart came the last bit of blood and water. And John said, "I have witnessed it, and my witness is true." Why? Out of the blood of our Lord Jesus and out of the life of our Lord Jesus He made His bride. It is His body today, His bride coming.

We are entrusted with this mystery. We are here on earth with a vision, with a trust from God Himself to build the church. That is our mission. We are to see that the body of Christ is being built. It is not a matter of our personal spirituality. God does not want monuments; He wants a house. He does not want individual giants; He wants a body, the body of Christ, and it is our responsibility to allow the Holy Spirit to use us to build that body.

What is the stewardship? In Ephesians 4:3 it says, "We ought to keep diligently the unity of the spirit in the uniting bond of peace." We need to fellowship with one another in spite of

differences. We need to be under the headship of
Christ. Hold fast the Head that all the members
may be united together and minister one to
another for the building up of the body in love.
This is our stewardship of the mystery of Christ.
Are we fulfilling it? Are we faithful and prudent
stewards of God's household?

The Mystery of Godliness

The third aspect of the mysteries of God is in
I Timothy 3:15-16 Paul says, "But if I delay, in
order that thou mayest know how one ought to
conduct oneself in God's house, which is the
church of the living God, the pillar and base of
the truth. And confessedly the mystery of piety
(or the mystery of godliness) is great, God (In
the original the word God is not there; it is Who.)
has been manifested in flesh, has been justified
in the Spirit, has appeared to angels, has been
preached among the nations, has been believed
on in the world, has been received up in glory."

The mystery of God is the mystery of
godliness. What is godliness? Godliness simply
means "like God." We have the life of God in us,
and it is the will of God that this should grow,

that this should grow more and more into conformity to the image of God's beloved Son. This is what the church is. This is our testimony.

And as people read these two verses they may wonder why the translator put the word *God* in it because in the original it is just *Who*, but they do not know who this *Who* is. And if you read on you will find *Who* is none other than God Himself. That is true, but if you really read the preceding verse, what is the antecedent of verse 16? The mystery of godliness is great. What does that mystery of godliness refer to? God is God, and there is nothing strange about God being godly, but here you find the mystery of godliness. Why is it a mystery? Because it was something unknown before, impossible, but now made possible. What is the mystery of godliness? If you read the former verse it talks about the church. The church is the mystery of godliness.

"Manifested in flesh..." The church is heavenly in nature but it is manifested in flesh upon this earth, and has been justified in the Spirit. It is the Spirit. In one Spirit we were baptized into one body, whether Jews or

Gentiles, and were all made to drink of one Spirit.

"Has appeared to angels..." The angels look at the church and wonder. They learn from the church the all-various wisdom of God, what God has done in this group who are men, lower than the angels, and God can make them like Christ. Isn't that marvelous?

"Has been preached among the nations..." We would say that we do not preach the church. If you preach the church you will get the cross. We preach Christ and you get the church. But thank God, so far as the world is concerned, the world should know what the church is.

"Has been believed on in the world..." In the early church you find people looking at the church and saying, "Who are they?" They are Christians. They were attracted to them and they believed,

"Has been received up to glory." The church is here in the wilderness on a journey. We are going to glory.

This is the mystery of godliness, and this is entrusted to us. How are we going to fulfill that trust?

In I Timothy 4:8-9: "Exercise thyself unto godliness; for bodily exercise is profitable for a little, but godliness is profitable for everything, having promise of life, of the present one, and of that to come. The word is faithful and worthy of all acceptation."

Brothers and sisters, how can we fulfill the trust, the responsibility, the managing of this mystery of godliness, unless we exercise godliness in our daily life. We know how to exercise our physical body. We are being told again and again how important it is that we should exercise for our health, for our well-being. But the Bible says, "Yes, it profits us a little, but to exercise godliness is not only for now but for eternity."

How can we exercise godliness? It is by cooperating with the Holy Spirit. The Holy Spirit within us teaches us in all things, and if we obey the teaching of the anointing within us, we abide in Christ. By abiding in Christ we become like Him. This is our responsibility. We must do it.

The Mystery of the Glad Tidings

And finally, the fourth aspect is in Ephesians 6:19: "And for me in order that utterance may be given to me in the opening of my mouth to make known with boldness the mystery of the glad tidings."

Colossians 1:24-29: "Now, I rejoice in sufferings for you, and I fill up that which is behind of the tribulations of Christ in my flesh, for his body, which is the church; of which I became minister, according to the dispensation of God which is given me towards you to complete the word of God, the mystery which has been hidden from ages and from generations, but has now been made manifest to his saints; to whom God would make known what are the riches of the glory of this mystery among the nations, which is Christ in you the hope of glory: whom we announce, admonishing every man, and teaching every man, in all wisdom, to the end that we may present every man perfect in Christ. Whereunto also I toil, combating according to his working, which works in me in power."

There is the mystery of the glad tidings, the mystery of the gospel. People have never thought of the gospel that God has prepared for man. It is beyond man's understanding. They think it is foolishness; it is weakness. But to us the cross is the wisdom of God, the power of God. Wonderful! "...and Christ in you the hope of glory."

These are the various aspects of the mysteries of God, and God so loves us, He has such faith in us that He entrusts all to us. What a responsibility! Who can fulfill this task? Thank God, we cannot, but He can. This is where grace comes in. It is a mystery. God's grace is so immense, so manifold, so complete that He is able to work in us all that He has entrusted to us. To God be the glory! Amen.

Dear Lord, we bow in worship that Thou should have such faith in us because Thou has faith in Thyself. Lord, we are unworthy, but Thy love has constrained us. We are willing. Use us to fulfill Thy eternal purpose. We ask in Thy name, Amen.

QUESTIONS & ANSWERS

Dear brothers and sisters, we hope this will not be a mental exercise, but God would turn it into a spiritual exercise. By the grace of God we hope that these intellectual questions will become our spiritual experience. Christ is the answer, and may we come into a more intimate, living, real fellowship with Him. And that is the purpose of this time.

I was given three questions; two are related to our theme, but one is a general one. I will try to answer them by the grace of God briefly.

Q: Please classify the distinction between a slave, son, and steward.

We are not referring to three different classes of people. When we are talking about slave or bondman, son, and steward, we are talking about the one and same person. It is just a description of the different aspects of our relationship with our Lord.

Our Lord gave Himself for us. He bought us with a price. Salvation is more than just getting saved, out of hell into heaven. Salvation is such that we are saved to be no longer ours but His. We are all bought with a price. We are all slaves, as it were, in a good sense, bondmen of Christ Jesus. We have no liberty of ourselves, no right to our lives. We are His. And our whole life is supposed to be the life of a bondslave. We love Him; we love His household. We will not go out free, but we want to be with Him and serve Him with all our hearts. That is our relationship with Him so far as redemption is concerned.

Thank God, we are not only slaves but we are sons because by the grace of God we are born from above. We have His very life in us, and this life is supposed to grow from children into sons. He that is led by the Spirit of God is the son of God. So in our lives we need to be led by the Spirit of God. If we are not led by the Spirit of God in our daily lives, we remain babes in Christ, and as babes in Christ we can never be a steward to the mysteries of God. So thank God, this life grows within us from childhood into manhood, and as sons that means the life that God has given to us is maturing. So that speaks of our life relationship with the Lord. And as the life is maturing, then in the measure of the maturing of His life in us comes the measure of our responsibility, our stewardship. And that is when we are able to fulfill our responsibility as stewards of the grace of God as well as the mysteries of God. So you find these three are closely related. They can be distinguished but they cannot be separated, and you are not just a bondslave, not just a son, but also a steward. That is what we all are. Thank God for that.

Q: How does this relate to eternal security? Are they different or separate issues? Please provide Scriptures.

A: A number of people are concerned with this matter of eternal security. We want to be secure, not only for this life but also for eternity. We are clever. Thank God, eternal security is something that God has promised us. Eternal security is not in us. If it is in us it will never be secure. But thank God, eternal security is God's eternal purpose for us.

Romans 8:29-30 says, "Because whom he has foreknown, he has also predestinated to be conformed to the image of his Son, so that he should be the firstborn among many brethren. But whom he has predestinated, these also he has called; and whom he has called, these also he has justified; but whom he has justified, these also he has glorified."

Then in Romans 11:29: "For the gifts and the calling of God are not subject to repentance."

Our eternal security is rooted in the eternal purpose of God. Can you have anything more secure than that? It is God's good pleasure. It is what He foreknows of us. According to His foreknowledge He has predestinated us to be conformed to the image of His beloved Son. And whom He has called He has justified, and whom He has justified He has glorified. It is His gift, and it is His calling. And His gift and calling has no repentance. He is not a baby or a child. When a child is friendly with His friends, he shares or even gives his toys to his friends. When he is unfriendly he wants everything back. This is not our God. Once He gives a gift, it is forever. Once

He has called us, He will keep us. So thank God, eternal security is in God, not in you, not in me.

And furthermore, eternal security is the grace of God. Ephesians 2:8: "For ye are saved by grace through faith, and this not of yourself; it is God's gift."

If it is the grace of God, it does not depend upon our behavior. If we behave well He saves us. If we do not behave, He takes away that salvation. That is man; that is not God. So we are secure in the grace of God.

Finally, we are secured in God's almighty power. John 10:28-29: "And I give them life eternal; and they shall never perish, and no one shall seize them out of my hand. My Father who has given them to me is greater than all, and no one can seize out of the hand of my Father."

Now with God the Son and God the Father both holding our hands we are secure. So thank God for eternal security.

Q: Then we have this matter on inheritance.

A: Inheritance is one of the biggest subjects in the Bible. We could spend a whole week on this matter of inheritance. So we are not able to deal with it fully at this time. Just let me quote one Scripture in Acts 26:18. Our Lord Jesus appeared to Saul of Tarsus on the road to Damascus and there we find His commission to Saul: "I send thee, to open their eyes, that they may turn from darkness to light, and from the power of Satan to God, that they may receive remission of sins and inheritance among them that are sanctified by faith in me."

We receive remission of sins; we have our sins forgiven, thank God for that. So far as we are concerned, we are redeemed, but also we are given the inheritance among them that are sanctified by faith in Him. It is like in Ruth. Our Kinsman-Redeemer comes and rescues us, redeems our inheritance, and even redeems our fallen man. So thank God for that. This matter of inheritance is wonderful.

Ephesians 1:13-14: "In whom ye also have trusted, having heard the word of the truth, the glad tidings of your salvation; in whom also, having believed, ye have been sealed with the Holy Spirit of promise."

Why sealed? "Who is the earnest of our inheritance to the redemption of the acquired possession to the praise of his glory."

V. 18: "Being enlightened in the eyes of your heart, so that ye should know what is the hope of his calling, and what the riches of the glory of his inheritance in the saints."

Christ is our inheritance, and our portion falls in the good ground. Wonderful! But the marvel is we are the inheritance of Christ. Christ our inheritance is glory. How glorious He is! And we have Him as our inheritance in fullness. Think of that! We become His inheritance and also the glory of His inheritance. His glory has transformed us. Wonderful!

This matter of stewardship and inheritance is closely related. If we are faithful and prudent stewards we will inherit with our Lord Jesus during the coming kingdom, the millennium age, to reign and rule with Christ for a thousand years. If we are unfaithful and foolish, we think we have a good time in our lives, we refuse to be disciplined, we refuse to suffer for Christ's sake, will we lose our inheritance? Yes and no. We will lose our inheritance in the age to come, which is the millennium age. Instead of coming into the banquet of the marriage feast of the Lamb, we are shut out in darkness, gnashing our teeth, regretting what we have done, foolish. But thank God, this is not punishment; this is discipline. And discipline is unto maturity. So somehow what God has predestined for us, in spite of us, grace will finish the work, and in eternity we all inherit the heavenly Jerusalem. Wonderful! On the one hand we need to be comforted; on the other hand, we need to be warned. For the sake of a few years, you can forfeit the glory of a thousand years. Is it worth it? So these two things are closely related.

Q: Sonship related to stewardship—is one necessary before the other?

A: Sonship and stewardship actually are one. When you are placing a son, it means you are in stewardship. If we are faithful in that which is not ours, He will give us ours to keep. If we are faithful in the little, He will give us much. So these two things are really very closely related. In the measure of sonship is the measure of stewardship.

Q: How can I spend more time with God? I try to do it but it always fails. How do you remember to spend time with God?

A: Now when you read this question, on the one hand you think that this brother or sister wants to have some time with God, but towards the last he says, "How can you remember to spend time with God?" Now if it is something that you can forget so quickly, it means that you do not really want it very eagerly. So I think the whole question is deeper than that. It is not a matter of spending time with the Lord; it is a matter of your consecration. It is a matter of your priority. Have you really given yourself totally without reserve according to all that you know? Have you presented your body a living sacrifice, wholly, acceptable to God which is your reasonable service? Have you done that? Are you doing it? Now if that is the case, then all your time is the Lord's. He is the priority. He has the first of your time, and if He is the first of your time it is very easy to find time to be with Him. So I think this is a deeper question. And may the Lord help us that we may be those who are totally committed to Him.

.

Other Books Printed By
Christian Testimony Ministry

SPEAKER	TITLE
DANA CONGDON	MARRIAGE, SINGLENESS, AND THE WILL OF GOD
	RECOVERY & RESTORATION
	THE HOLY SPIRIT
	HEBREWS
A.J. FLACK	TENT OF HIS SPLENDOUR
STEPHEN KAUNG	ACTS
	BE YE THEREFORE PERFECT
	CALLED OUT UNTO CHRIST
	CALLED TO THE FELLOWSHIP OF GOD'S SON
	DIVINE LIFE AND ORDER
	FOR ME TO LIVE IS CHRIST
	GLORIOUS LIBERTY OF THE CHILDREN OF GOD
	GOD'S PURPOSE FOR THE FAMILY
	I WILL BUILD MY CHURCH
	MEDITATIONS ON THE KINGDOM
	RECOVERY
	SPIRITUAL EXERCISE
	SPIRITUAL LIFE (II CORINTHIANS SERIES)
	TEACH US TO PRAY
	THE CROSS
	THE FULNESS OF CHRIST—IN THE BOOK OF REVELATION
	THE HEADSHIP OF CHRIST
	THE KINGDOM AND THE CHURCH
	THE KINGDOM OF GOD
	THE LAST CALL TO THE CHURCHES, THE CALL TO OVERCOME
	THE LIFE OF OUR LORD JESUS
	THE LIFE OF THE CHURCH, THE BODY OF CHRIST
	THE LORD'S TABLE
	TWO GUIDEPOSTS FOR INHERITING THE KINGDOM
	VISION OF CHRIST (REVELATION)
	WHO ARE WE?

WHY DO WE SO GATHER?
WORSHIP

LANCE LAMBERT

CALLED UNTO HIS ETERNAL GLORY
GOD'S ETERNAL PURPOSE
IN THE DAY OF THY POWER
JACOB I HAVE LOVED
LIVING FAITH
LESSONS FROM THE LIFE OF MOSES
LOVE DIVINE
MY HOUSE SHALL BE A HOUSE OF PRAYER
PREPARATION FOR THE COMING OF THE LORD
REIGNING WITH CHRIST
SPIRITUAL CHARACTER
THE GOSPEL OF THE KINGDOM
THE IMPORTANCE OF COVERING
THE LAST DAYS AND GOD'S PRIORITIES
THE PRIZE
THE SUPREMACY OF JESUS CHRIST
THINE IS THE POWER!
THOU ART MINE

T. AUSTIN-SPARKS

THE LORD'S TESTIMONY AND THE WORLD NEED

HARVEY CEDARS CONFERENCE

STEPHEN KAUNG

HEAVENLY VISION
SPIRITUAL RESPONSIBILITY

CONGDON, HILE, KAUNG

SPIRITUAL MINISTRY
SPIRITUAL AUTHORITY
SPIRITUAL HOUSE
SPIRITUAL SUBMISSION

STEPHEN KAUNG

SPIRITUAL KNOWLEDGE
SPIRITUAL POWER
SPIRITUAL REALITY
SPIRITUAL VALUE
SPIRITUAL BLESSING
SPIRITUAL DISCERNMENT

SPIRITUAL WARFARE
SPIRITUAL ASCENDANCY
SPIRITUAL MINDEDNESS
SPIRITUAL PERFECTION
SPIRITUAL FULNESS
SPIRITUAL SONSHIP
SPIRITUAL STEWARDSHIP
SPIRITUAL TRAVAIL
SPIRITUAL INHERITANCE
HARVEY CEDARS CONFERENCE:
HILE, KAUNG, LAMBERT
THE KING IS COMING

www.ingramcontent.com/pod-product-compliance
Lightning Source LLC
Chambersburg PA
CBHW060708030426
42337CB00017B/2795